FROM GLASS
To Boat

A Photo Essay
by Cindy Purcell

Children's Press

A Division of Grolier Publishing
New York London Hong Kong Sydney
Danbury, Connecticut

Created and Developed by The Learning Source

Designed by Josh Simons

Acknowledgments: The Learning Source would like to thank Wendi Silcott and Tiffany Henderson of Owens Corning and Rick Hopp of Fiberglass Coatings, Inc., for all their help. Also, a huge thanks goes to Benham Purcell of Huckins Yacht for her assistance and support with this project.

Photo Credits: Bombardier Inc.: 32 (middle, left), (top, right); Huckins Yacht Corporation: cover (inset), 1, 3, 12-31; Jamaica Tourist Board: 5, 7, 32 (top, left), (bottom, right), (middle, right); Owens Corning: cover (background), 2, 9, 10, 11; Josh Simons/The Learning Source: 8; SuperStock, Inc.: 4, 6, 32 (bottom, left).

Note: The actual boatmaking process often varies from manufacturer to manufacturer. The process described in this book is representative of one of the most common methods of building boats today.

Library of Congress Cataloging-in-Publication Data
Purcell, Cindy.
     From glass to boat : a photo essay / by Cindy Purcell.
        p.   cm. — (Changes)
Summary: Describes the process by which fiberglass boats are made, from the melting of glass marbles to create the fiberglass to the molding and finishing of the boat.
ISBN 0-516-20736-9 (lib.bdg.)   0-516-20367-3 (pbk.)
     1. Fiberglass boats—Design and construction—Juvenile literature. [1. Fiberglass boats. 2. Boats and boating.] I. Title. II. Series: Changes (New York, N.Y.)
VM321.P87   1997
623. 8'458—dc21   97-22706 CIP
                                  AC

Printed in the United States of America
1 2 3 4 5 6 7 8 9 10 R 06 05 04 03 02 01 00 99 98 97

Long before there were trains, automobiles, or planes, boats sailed the waters.

People used boats for working, trading, exploring, and of course, for fishing. Today, boats are used for all this and more.

Whether it's for fun in the sun or the catch of the day . . .

. . . people love to spend time on boats.

But how are boats made?

Most modern-day boats begin with glass marbles like these. When they are heated and then melted, the marbles turn into thin strands—like spaghetti—called fiberglass.

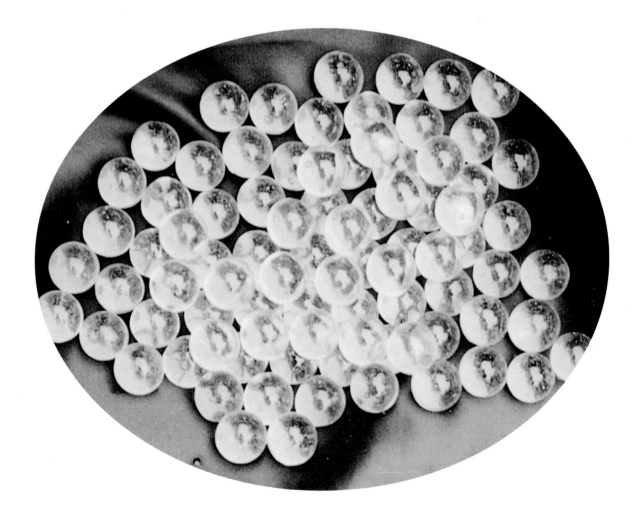

Next, a spinning drum catches the hot glass fibers and wraps them, like thread, around spools.

Once cool, many fiberglass strands are twisted together into yarn.

Afterward, machines weave the yarn into a kind of cloth that is sent to the boat factory.

Meanwhile, at the boat factory, workers are busy creating a wooden jig, or skeleton, of the boat's hull. The hull is the watertight, main body of a boat.

Now sheets of thin plywood are put over the jig
to make a mold.

Wax is spread over the mold. Later on, this will help workers separate the mold from the finished hull.

Then layer after layer of foam padding and fiberglass . . .

. . . are glued and tacked down to the mold.
Together, the layers make a sturdy, light hull.

While the hull is still upside down, workers make sure the surface is flat and smooth.

Looking for dips and dents is not easy because the hull is more than 60 feet (18 meters) in length. That's longer than a humpback whale!

Once the hull is ready, it is hauled outside. There, big cranes turn it right side up.

Next, workers strip away the wooden mold . . .

. . . and lay down floor supports from one end of the hull to the other.

Walls called bulkheads go in, dividing the hull into separate rooms and compartments.

Finished rooms are made as comfortable and cozy
as ones at home.

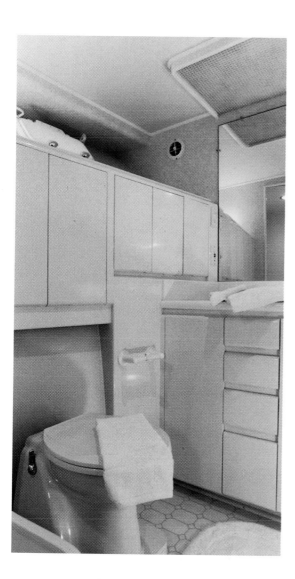

Then in go the decks and on goes the top.
But this boat is far from ready.

It still needs engines and propellers, which fit into the bottom of the hull.

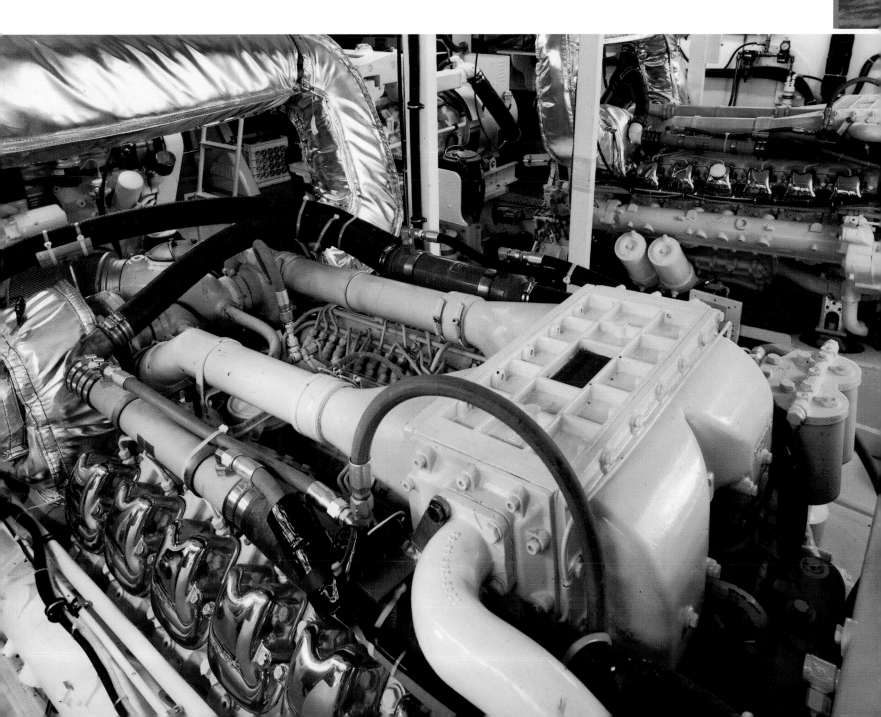

Above deck, too, there is work to be done. Radar, radios, and other instruments must be installed in the bridge. This is where the boat is steered.

When everything else is in place, paint and polish add the finishing touch just before . . .

. . . the boat sails away.

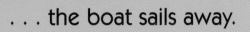

Bon voyage!

Here are some other kinds of
watercraft made of fiberglass.
Which ones would you like to try?

 Sloop

 Jet ski

 Jet boat

 Decked Canoe

 Runabout

 Catamaran